R.H-K: For my Gaga and Grumps. You mean the world to me. And for ALL the children who have ever felt like nobody cares – I do!

N.S: For Rico

BLOOMSBURY CHILDREN'S BOOKS
Bloomsbury Publishing Plc
50 Bedford Square, London, WC1B 3DP, UK
29 Earlsfort Terrace, Dublin 2, Ireland

BLOOMSBURY, BLOOMSBURY CHILDREN'S BOOKS and the Diana logo are trademarks of Bloomsbury Publishing Plc

First published in Great Britain 2022 by Bloomsbury Publishing Plc

Text copyright © Rico Hinson-King, 2022 Illustrations copyright © Nick Sharratt, 2022

Rico Hinson-King and Nick Sharratt have asserted their right under the Copyright, Designs and Patents Act, 1988, to be identified as Author and Illustrator of this work

A catalogue record for this book is available from the British Library

ISBN: HB: 978-1-5266-4862-4; PB: 978-1-5266-4863-1; eBook: 978-1-5266-5265-2

2 4 6 8 10 9 7 5 3 1

Printed and bound in Italy by Graphicom Spa

FSC
www.fsc.org
MIX
Paper from responsible sources
FSC® C013123

To find out more about our authors and books visit www.bloomsbury.com and sign up for our newsletters

This is Charlie's personal foster care journey but not every child's story will be the same. We recommend reading and reflecting on this book with a grown-up.

GLOSSARY

☆ **Adoption:** When a person or couple becomes a parent to a child who can no longer live with their birth parents

☆ **Birth family:** The family you are born into

☆ **Contact centre:** A safe place where children can meet family members they don't live with

☆ **Foster home:** A safe place for children to stay that isn't with their birth parents

☆ **Foster parent:** Someone who takes a child into their family to look after them for a while

☆ **Judge:** A person who is in charge of making important decisions

☆ **Social worker:** A person who helps children, adults and families with problems

Look out for these terms in bold throughout the book.

Rico Hinson-King

Nick Sharratt

STRONG AND TOUGH

BLOOMSBURY
CHILDREN'S BOOKS
LONDON   OXFORD   NEW YORK   NEW DELHI   SYDNEY

There was a kid. Let's call him Charlie.

On the outside, he looked like every other **football-mad** boy of his age.

But he wasn't ...

Charlie's life hadn't always been great. When he was very small, his **birth parents** couldn't look after him or his sisters.

Some people called **social workers** came to take Charlie to a **foster home** where he would be **safe**.

Charlie's sisters were taken to a **foster home** too, but **not the same one as Charlie**.

It was **REALLY** scary.

I wish I knew what was going on ...

Charlie's foster home was nice, but it was **new** and **strange**. He had a small room all to himself, with a few toys to play with. But there was no garden to play football in.

Charlie missed being with his sisters. Alone and afraid, he cried sometimes, but he was **determined to be strong**.

As the weeks went by, he met lots of **social workers**.

He didn't know how long he'd be
staying at the **foster home** or if he
would see his **birth parents** again.

Charlie saw his two sisters each week. On some days they met in a building called a **contact centre**. All they could do was play board games and talk.

Charlie was always really sad when he had to say goodbye. But he never complained. **He was strong. He was tough.**

On other days they went to the park and played football.
This was **MUCH** more fun. Charlie **loved** those days.

Charlie's **foster parent** encouraged him to talk about his feelings — and sometimes Charlie did — but all he really wanted was a **forever family** and nobody talked to him about *that*.

One day, a **social worker** told Charlie that two **foster parents** were going to look after him AND his two sisters until a wise person, called the **judge**, decided what would happen to them.

Charlie was so **excited**.
Finally, he would live with his sisters!

But he was a little nervous too ...

And there was an excited
floppy-eared puppy named Belle.
Charlie had always wanted a pet!

But, **best of all**, Charlie's sisters were there too! He ran into their arms and hugged them tight. He didn't **ever** want to let go.

Charlie felt happy, but still he kept worrying.
He didn't know how long he'd be able to stay,
or if he'd be split up from his sisters again.
As always, he tried to be brave.

He was **strong**. He was **tough**.

Months went by, and Charlie and his sisters were **happy** and **safe**.
Their **foster parents** let them do lots of fun, new things.

They went on walks

and had picnics in the park.

They bounced **high** on their trampoline.

And Charlie even learnt how to swim.

He felt **normal**.

Although on the inside
Charlie still had to work
hard to stay strong.

Finally, the **judge** decided that Charlie would not be able to go back to his **birth family** and that he and his sisters were going to be **adopted**.

At first, Charlie was happy. He would finally have a **forever family**! But then the **social worker** told him that the chances of him and his sisters staying together were almost impossible.

Charlie wanted to

SCREAM AND CRY!

And he did.
A little.

But Charlie didn't give up hope. **He was strong**. **He was tough**.
Football helped take his mind off things. So, he played every day.

In the park …

in the garden …

and even in the house!

Soon he had managed to get the **whole family** to play as a team.

Then it happened ...

On the same day he scored the winning goal in a football match, a **social worker** sat him down and explained that his **foster parents** had asked if they could **adopt Charlie** and **his sisters**!

It was like scoring the winning, sudden-death penalty in a cup final.

Charlie was so SO happy
that he thought he might

BURST!

He had a **forever family** and it was **EXTRA SPECIAL** because his new parents had *chosen* him.

Oh, and in case you're wondering, Charlie is doing really well in **life** and in **football**.

How do I know?

Ah, that's easy, because **I am Charlie**.

RICO